# ALVIN LUCIER

## A Celebration

with an introduction by Michael S. Roth

essays by Nicolas Collins and Ronald Kuivila

and an interview

with Andrea Miller-Keller and Alvin Lucier

Published in conjunction with the exhibition
*Alvin Lucier (and His Artist Friends)*
at the Ezra and Cecile Zilkha Gallery, Wesleyan University
November 4 through December 11, 2011

Wesleyan University Press
Middletown, Connecticut 06459
www.wesleyan.edu/wespress

Manufactured in the United States of America

Library of Congress Cataloging-in-Publication Data
Alvin Lucier : a celebration / with an introduction
by Michael S. Roth ; essays by Nicolas Collins and Ronald Kuivila
and an interview with Andrea Miller-Keller and Alvin Lucier.
      p. cm.
 Includes bibliographical references.
 ISBN 978–0–8195–7279–0 (pbk. : alk. paper) —
 ISBN 978–0–8195–7280–6 (ebook)
1.  Lucier, Alvin. 2.  Composers — United States —
Biography.  I. Collins, Nicolas. II. Kuivila, Ron.
III. Miller-Keller, Andrea.
 ML410.L8973A65 2011
 780.92 — dc23
                        2011039041

5 4 3 2 1

Editor: Andrea Miller-Keller
Design and typography: Catherine Waters
Production and press supervision: The Production Department
Printing and binding: The Studley Press Inc.

*Back cover image*:
Alvin Lucier, Rezonanzen Festival, Berlin, 1999
Photo credit: Michael Schroedter

# Table of Contents

Alvin Lucier, Parshall, Colorado, 1997
Photo credit: Amanda Lucier

# Introduction

Michael S. Roth
*President, Wesleyan University*

What a gift, what a pleasure to celebrate the musical contributions of Alvin Lucier, who has been inspiring students at Wesleyan since 1968. When he started teaching here, Alvin was joining a department that already had demonstrated a strong commitment to experimental and world music. John Cage had made Wesleyan a home away from home, and David McAllester, Bob Brown and Richard Winslow were bringing sounds from around the world (and the instruments that make them) to this quiet campus in central Connecticut. But perhaps "quiet" is the wrong word. After all, revolutionary campus politics and avant-garde ideas were animating the Wesleyan culture when Alvin began teaching here. He, too, was open to revolutionary and avant-garde impulses; and he was also open to the possibilities for hearing things within the quiet. It turned out to be an enormously potent combination.

At Wesleyan, Alvin's anti-parochialism found fertile soil. There were always willing musical collaborators, and visual artists, too, found inspiration in his spirit and his practice. Disciplinary constraints make little sense to artists or to scientists, and at Wesleyan we have tried to cultivate a spirit of experimentation that responds to what is happening in the world—not to what is expected from convention.

Alvin Lucier's contributions to experimental music have continued to produce what we most hope for from the best forms of experimentation: opening us up to new ways of thinking/feeling and shaking up what we thought we already knew. Each year students have entered his classes thinking they know what music is, where it comes from and even what it might be. Without hectoring, without preaching, they are taught to think otherwise. What a gift! What a pleasure!

Alvin Lucier, *Music for Pure Waves,*
*Bass Drums and Acoustic Pendulums,* (1980)
Crowell Concert Hall,
Wesleyan University, 1985
Photo credit: Gary Smith

## In Appreciation

Pamela Tatge
*Director, Center for the Arts,*
*Wesleyan University*

On behalf of the faculty, staff and students affiliated with Wesleyan's Center for the Arts, we are delighted to offer this catalog in tribute to the widely acclaimed Alvin Lucier, known affectionately to many of us here at Wesleyan simply as Alvin.

A liberal arts education is the opportunity to expand one's world-view, and at Wesleyan the arts are seen as an essential component of this exploration. Alvin's work on our stages and in our classrooms has played a unique role in this exploration. When the music department invited Alvin to join the faculty in 1968, they dedicated themselves to a curriculum that would celebrate experimentation and innovation, a reputation they have admirably developed and strengthened ever since. Over the past forty years Alvin has taught several thousand undergraduate and graduate students, many of whom he has influenced in immeasurable ways. Throughout an era in which logic, information, competition and ambition hold sway, Alvin has embodied a different set of values. He has been a generous and giving professor, challenging his students intellectually while also giving them the space and the freedom to allow their imaginations to flourish.

Alvin's intellect, his disarming sense of humor and his infectious *joie de vivre* are widely cherished. Few of us who know him would ever casually pass Alvin in the CFA courtyard. Rather, we are eager to stop and hear about the latest trip, the most recent concert or the witty observation that will undoubtedly send us on our way feeling enriched and fortunate to have crossed paths with him once again.

A gifted practicing artist who has toured the world, Alvin has connected us with the new, the surprising and the compelling. We at Wesleyan University have known for a long time how very lucky we are to have such a historically significant and accomplished artist in our midst, one who has also been a devoted and engaged teacher on campus. Such distinguished figures are more often imported for a one-year residency. Wesleyan has had Alvin "in residence" and active on our campus for *four decades*, and for this we are so grateful.

John Cage and Alvin Lucier preparing for
Christian Wolff's *For 1, 2, or 3 People,* (1964)
Cage Symposium, Wesleyan University, 1988
Photo credit: Nancy Walz

# Symposium

**Notations**

November 4, 2011 from 12:15pm–2pm

CFA Hall

Since the composition of *Crossings* (1982–1984), Alvin Lucier has devoted much attention to composing pieces for instrumentalists. In all of these works, the actions of the performer serve more to expose the sonic phenomenon that is the central focus of the piece than to enact an expressive gesture. The same sensibility underlies Lucier's prose works, even those that can invite quite theatrical realization. This panel explores the commitment to *sounding* over *shaping,* and how it and related issues can inform the performance of music.

*Anthony Burr*

*Volker Straebel*

*Daniel Wolf*

*Moderator: Jane Alden*

**Processes**

November 4, 2011 from 2:30pm–4pm

CFA Hall

Alvin Lucier's electronic music has always avoided the conventions of electroacoustic music in various ways, including the amplification of brain waves, the use of small pulse streams physically moved through a space, the repeated rerecording of a sound in a space or the use of a pure tone to resonate percussion instruments. Lucier chooses instead to use electronic and acoustical processes to reveal relations to sound that have not been previously enacted in music. This panel will discuss those processes and the threads they form throughout his oeuvre.

*Nicolas Collins*

*Andrew Dewar*

*Hauke Harder*

*Moderator: Neely Bruce*

9

**Performance**

November 5, 2011 from 10am–11:30am

CFA Hall

In the early 1960s, Alvin Lucier departed from his training as a neoclassical composer and became an active participant in the lively community of artists, composers and choreographers that congregated around the Judson Church in New York City, the ONCE Festival in Ann Arbor, Michigan and the San Francisco Tape Music Center. The Performance panel will explore these origins, the pieces he made during that time, and their influences on his subsequent work.

*Charles Curtis*

*Ronald Kuivila*

*Richard Lerman*

*Moderator: Mark Slobin*


**Composers' Roundtable**

November 6, 2011 from 11am–12:30pm

CFA Hall

This panel brings together close colleagues and younger composers to share their insights and questions relating to Alvin Lucier and his work.

*Robert Ashley*

*David Behrman*

*Paula Matthusen*

*Gordon Mumma*

*Pauline Oliveros*

*Christian Wolff*

*Moderator: Anthony Braxton*

**Screenings**

*No Ideas But In Things*
Viola Rusche and Hauke Harder, 2012, 96 minutes
November 4, 2011 at 4:30pm
CFA Hall

This documentary on Alvin Lucier's work and teaching will be premiered in Berlin in the spring of 2012. This sneak preview screening will be introduced by the documentary's makers, Rusche and Harder.

*Tribute to John Cage*
Nam June Paik,1972, 60 minutes
November 5, 2011 at 12pm
CFA Hall

This tribute to John Cage's 60th birthday features an extended performance by Alvin Lucier as an "expert" on the music of John Cage. John Hanhardt, senior curator at the Smithsonian Museum of American Art and formerly at the Whitney Museum, will introduce the screening. Hanhardt was one of the first curators to introduce sound works to gallery exhibitions.

Nicolas Collins and his mother, Christiane,
with Alvin Lucier, Commencement,
Wesleyan University, May 1976
Photo credit: George and Luke Collins

# Vespers

Nicolas Collins

One of the peculiar charms of American universities is their warm embrace of the clueless applicant. In most countries, admission to higher education is predicated on one's having a pretty clear idea of a specific course of study. American colleges, by contrast, have a fondness for the applicant who avows passion for physics, poetry and pottery in equal measure. I was one of those typical confused 18-year-old souls when I arrived at Wesleyan in 1972. Alvin Lucier's *Vespers* saved me.

On an April day midway through my second semester, Lucier presented his composition *Vespers* as part of his Introduction to Electronic Music course. He handed four of us blindfolds and flashlight-shaped electronic instruments called "Sondols," and dimmed the lights. We shuffled awkwardly through the darkness, the Sondols emitting streams of sharp clicks. Aiming the instruments around the room and listening to the sounds reflect off the walls and furniture, we were told to navigate across the space by echolocation, in emulation of bats. We could switch the devices on and off and change the speed of the clicks, but the output of the Sondol was otherwise unvarying and, to be honest, musically unpromising. Listening carefully, however, I found that the echoes coalesced into a richly detailed, ever-changing, immersive cloud that hung in the air—a stippled sonic portrait of the architecture in which we stood. Most of the electronic music I knew came from a pair of loudspeakers—*Vespers* came from everywhere. This was more than just the weirdest, coolest music I had ever heard; it changed all my assumptions of what music—and composers—could be.

A native New Yorker, I was no stranger to the avant-garde. My mother still waxes nostalgic about taking me to Stockhausen and Ives concerts when I was a tot, although I displayed a consistent lack of musical talent from grade-school recorder classes through teenage flirtations with electric guitar. I was, however, a fanatical music consumer—mostly pop, blues, some jazz and "world music"— and at age 17, I bought a secondhand Tandberg reel-to-reel tape recorder to dub radio broadcasts and my friends' records. As it happens, this machine contained a hidden, undocumented switch that, when thrown, induced delicious, semi-controllable swoops of feedback. I was smitten by the siren call of electronic sound.

A Moog was way beyond reach, but a simple oscillator could be had for the cost of a soldering iron, an integrated circuit from a touch-tone telephone and a copy of a hobby magazine. I gradually picked up enough electronic technique from books and magazines to accomplish the engineer's equivalent of ordering a beer in a foreign bar. My understanding of Serious Music, however, was hobbled by the fact that I still felt more comfortable at the Fillmore than the Philharmonic. Bach, Bartók and Berio lived on the other side of an ocean, they spoke another language, and I knew I was missing their nuances and jokes. I simply didn't have the intuition for European classical music that I had for the rest of my audio world. So while I worked hard to learn as much music theory as possible, I worried that at 17 I was already too old to become truly fluent.

Thus, my first year at Wesleyan I studied archaeology, linguistics, history of science, studio art, geology and tabla. This academic smorgasbord was an accurate portrait of my mind at the time. My advisor, Jon Barlow, encouraged me to enroll in Lucier's class, promising "he makes music with bats and porpoises." I signed up.

It was my entrée to the work of John Cage, Morton Feldman, Earle Brown, Christian Wolff, David Tudor, Terry Riley, LaMonte Young, Steve Reich, Philip Glass, Pauline Oliveros, the Sonic Arts Union—serious non-pop voices from my side of the ocean. Even for a smart-ass kid from New York this was an ear-opening experience. But nothing quite prepared me for *Vespers*.

To perform *Vespers* is to experience sound as survival rather than as self-expression or mere entertainment. At the same time, in its engagement with fundamental acoustics, the piece evokes the kind of ineffable axiomatic musicality I associate with strict species counterpoint. Earlier in the semester, Lucier had introduced Glass's *Music in Parallel Fifths* as a "return to the year zero" in Western music: going back to the first rule of counterpoint, violating it, and seeing what kind of music would evolve along this new branch. In *Vespers*, Lucier reached back even further, to a pre-hominid time before the divarication of music from all other sound, and he invented something that re-connected music to physics, architecture, animal behavior and social interaction—subjects that had intrigued me since childhood, but that I had never directly associated with music. *Vespers* seemed to tell me that I could make music about anything, not just some finite set of concepts handed down by the European classical lineage, that composition was not an activity bound by five lines, but an amorphous glue that could hold together my disparate interests.

I went on to study with Lucier for six years. Other works of his (most notably *I Am Sitting in a Room*) had a profound influence on my own style, and I could not have acquired a more thorough grounding in post-Cagean avant-garde than I did in Lucier's introductory class; but *Vespers* was my watershed. From that moment on, the fact that bats excited me more than Boulez vanished as an impediment. I could be a composer.

*This article first appeared in* The Wire *magazine issue 312 February 2010. Reproduced by permission. http://www.thewire.co.uk*

Alvin Lucier and Ron Kuivila, 1992
Photo credit: Bill Burkhart
Courtesy Wesleyan University Library,
Special Collections & Archives

# Alvin in Albany

Ronald Kuivila

I first encountered Alvin Lucier in 1972, as a high school student. I attended a SUNY Albany screening of Nam June Paik's *A Tribute to John Cage,* celebrating Cage's 60th birthday. One feature in this post-Fluxus vaudeville is an interview between WGBH's Russell Connor and Professor Alvin Lucier of Wesleyan University. In the interview, the professor, introduced as an expert on the music of John Cage, expounds knowledgeably, if a bit pedantically, on Cage's work. However, he makes no effort—whatsoever—to control his considerable stutter. The resultant text/sound composition, which includes many minutes of a sibilants never quite moving on to their subsequent vowels, was a bit terrifying for this untutored 16-year-old. But the sentences, when they would finally arrive, were clear, concise and often witty. And there were knowing chuckles from other audience members. So, I was gradually led to realize that all was not as it seemed and that, while the professor was not *pretending* to stutter, he was *electing* to stutter. Legend has it that, at the first screening, Cage turned to Alvin and informed him that he had decided he was the only person who should ever be allowed to lecture on his music.

Of course, this wonderfully compressed lesson in experimental music as *actions* rather than *acting*, as a *sounding* rather than a *shaping*, went mostly over my head. But it was unsettling, provoking and fascinating, and it left a mark. Six months later, when I found the professor's photo in a college catalog, I decided to apply to Wesleyan. It must be one of the most unlikely stories in the annals of college recruiting. Later, as an "admit," I came down to Wesleyan and attended a session of Alvin's signature course, Introduction to Experimental Music. He lectured on *Vespers*, his piece titled after bats of the family *Vespertilionidae.* He described his fascination with the natural sonar of bats as they echolocate themselves around obstacles and towards food and explained that treating the sound of bats as an *objet sonore* for tape manipulation seemed irrelevant to his real interest in echolocation itself. He then introduced a Sondol, a kind of sonic flashlight that produces a focused stream of sonic pulses at a variable rate. He explained that the device was intended to enable the blind to use a more refined form of echolocation than is possible with a cane. He then described how *Vespers* is performed: four musicians are asked to use echolocation to navigate from the corners of the concert space to an agreed location. He immediately acknowledged his own anxiety that the performance instructions were "too simple." The originality of the piece and the openness of his disclaimer told a powerful story echoed in just about every other lecture in that introductory course. Those stories have encouraged any number of young composers, artists and choreographers to follow their own paths as artists by asking questions and taking chances.

Alvin's own path into live electronic music was spurred by John Cage's insistence that he contribute a performance of "his brain wave piece" (ultimately entitled *Music for Solo Performer*) for a concert featuring the premier of Cage's *Rozart Mix*. Based on that experience, Lucier has always insisted that his students perform their work, irrespective of their level of confidence. It is more important to make discoveries than to avoid mistakes. From such starting points, Alvin has always been a master of providing small, practical suggestions that gently remove the extraneous choices young composers often make. You can see this at work in the new documentary *No Ideas But In Things*, previewed during this festival.

Viola Farber remarked that the simple humanity of the performers' actions in Alvin Lucier's live electronic music led her to invite him to be the music director for her dance company. She may have been thinking of the hesitant walk of a performer in *Vespers* guided only by the subtle changes of an echo. Of course, *Vespers* also refers to evening prayers of the Catholic liturgy. The outward focus of the performers as they listen for their echoes combines with their slow progression through the space to reinforce a vaguely ecclesiastical feeling, as if evening prayer has become a kind of sonic animism. The sly wit he brings to managing these associations can be discovered in other pieces focused on sound as a spatial phenomenon. In *Outlines of Persons and Things* a microphone appears to be both a sensor detecting the diffraction patterns of a high-pitched pure tone and a censer diffusing those variations as sonic incense. In *Bird And Person Dyning* the performer searches for feedback in tune with the call of a birdsong Christmas ornament in order to create different tones that appear to fly around each listener. Wearing a binaural microphone tethered to the sound system and garbed in down vest and duck waders straight from the L.L. Bean catalog, Alvin manages to elide a nature walk and lunar exploration in a manner that is vaguely preposterous but utterly effective.

Alvin commented in one seminar, that he "overdid" the editing on the LP recording of *Vespers* and tried to make the piece "too musical" in a superficial way. This comment captures the creative problem that underlies his work: how to compose musical, but unmannered encounters, with sound. In his live electronic work, this almost invariably involves simple but strikingly original technological configurations or actions. Since the composition of *Crossings*, Alvin has refocused on writing music for instrumentalists and singers. This makes the unmannered encounter even more difficult to attain as the old allegiances of musical tradition are inescapably co-present. He has found and continues to find a remarkable variety of solutions. In all of them, I detect a trace of *Vespers*: the music we hear is activated rather than expressed by the performer. Their job is not to shape their sounds so much as to reveal shapes already in the sounds. This is an exacting task that, when done well, reveals to us the simple humanity of devoting one's attention to sound.

*Music for Solo Performer*, (1965)
Lovely Music Album Cover, 1982
Photo credit: David A. Contor
Courtesy of Lovely Music, Ltd.

## The Early Years: Excerpts from an interview with Alvin Lucier

Interviewer: Andrea Miller-Keller

**AMK:** There is much intelligent, thoughtful material written about your work. And, you have written about it so clearly and extensively. However, covered to a lesser extent are your early years—your childhood and adolescence in Nashua, New Hampshire, your time as a student at Yale, Tanglewood and Brandeis, where you subsequently assumed your first academic position as Director of Choral Music in 1962. That was your last stop before arriving to teach at Wesleyan part-time in the fall of 1968 and then full-time in 1970. Both of your parents were musical, and you valued growing up in a musical household. Can you say more about that?

**AL:** My first memory of music was hearing my mother and father playing popular music at home. My father was an amateur violinist. As a boy he had studied with a member of the Boston Symphony, and it was up in the air whether he would go into music or become a lawyer. He finally became a lawyer and the mayor of Nashua, New Hampshire for two terms in the thirties, but he was always fond of jazz, such as it was in the teens and twenties. He graduated from Dartmouth in 1918, where he had organized a band later called the Barbary Coast Orchestra.

**AMK:** Dartmouth is still home to the Barbary Coast Jazz Ensemble!

**AL:** Yes, I don't think the term "jazz" had come into use at that time. My father was a classically trained player, but also a good improviser.

In high school my mother played piano for silent films in local movie theaters. She also, with her sister Louise (violin) and her brother John (drums), had a small dance band called the Lemery Trio. Can you believe that? They would play for all sorts of events—dances, wedding receptions. Once they were asked to play at a bar mitzvah. This must have been about 1915 or so. When the trio would add instruments for certain larger engagements, my father would sit in. I guess that's when their romance developed.

And the parties at my house...you can imagine! We had a gracious home, and there would always be a small orchestra playing: my father, a couple of friends on piano and guitar. *Blue Skies, Honeysuckle Rose*, songs like that. Really wonderful playing!

So at a very early age it became a major part of my mythology, but behind it all was a belief that there was a higher kind of music. What they meant by that was probably semi-classical music. My father used to mention Sibelius, but he really loved George Gershwin.

I remember the whole family sitting around the dinner table at night singing. My mother and my sisters would split up the soprano and alto parts and my father would sing bass. I would try to improvise the tenor part. This experience was wonderful.

I also remember that before I ever knew anything about notes—maybe at the age of five or six—writing down a bunch of dots on a piece of music paper, and my mother would sit down and play beautiful melodies and arpeggios, pretending that that was what I had written.

In high school I wrote a school song, but barely knew how to put the notes down on the page. I remember going into Boston and buying Walter Piston's book, *Harmonic Analysis*, and trying to figure it out.

**AMK:** So, you wanted to be a composer even before you knew much about music. And with this rich background you went on to make music your profession?

**AL:** I think what was more important than that was that my mother and father put such a premium on music. There was never doubt that being a musician or an artist was a high form of activity. It was never stated, but I think—this may be wrong—my sisters and I felt that our father might have been better off pursuing a career in music than being a lawyer and a politician. He was mayor of Nashua for two terms, but he didn't succeed in politics as he had hoped. He was defeated

**Technology is just one tool after another....I don't think of technology as technology....I think of it as the landscape....We're all born into a landscape....A 19th-century composer is talking about the 19th-century landscape... and I'm just responding to the landscape of my time.[1]**

*....Often, when I'm writing a piece, I have to de-compose. I have to not compose. I have all these ideas about the piece that come from composition that you study. I have to eliminate those things that distract from the acoustical unfolding of the idea....I have to work hard to put it in a form that allows it to reveal the magical quality it has without the interference of other ideas that don't fit in.* [2]

for Congress and Senate in New Hampshire, a heavily Republican state, and wasn't as happy at the end of his life as he might have been.

**AMK:** That's interesting because in your senior year at Yale, you, too, came to something of a crossroads.

**AL:** At Yale I took a course in Constitutional Law. I remember not studying hard in this class, but for some reason I did very well on the exam. The questions were to write briefs on various fictitious cases, referring to precedents.

I was intimidated by the other students, who were extremely confident in speaking up in class. I think Dick Thornburgh, later the Attorney General under Reagan and Bush, was in that class. The instructor called on everybody in alphabetical order, so when the "L's" came around I skipped class to avoid stuttering in front of these terribly verbal guys. However, I did well enough otherwise that the professor urged me to apply to Yale Law School. But finally I went for music.

**AMK:** Going back a bit, your first ambition was to be a jazz musician.

**AL:** Yes, I used to buy *Downbeat*, and listen to Stan Kenton, Count Basie and all those orchestras. I knew all the players as well as other boys knew athletes. I wanted to be a jazz musician, but much to my parents' consternation I didn't want to study the piano.

I had a set of drums in my basement and used to practice a lot. It's funny because the music I make now doesn't have much rhythm in it. I'm not a rhythmic composer. The only piece that comes to mind that was influenced by my study of drumming was my brain wave piece, *Music for Solo Performer*, which I made in 1965. In that piece I use enormously amplified alpha waves to resonate snare drums, bass drums, cymbals, gongs, all kinds of percussive instruments.

**AMK:** Yes, but so many of your other works are set up to reveal to the listener hidden beating patterns or resonances that are usually barely audible. This has been a deep and ongoing fascination for you. And almost all of your works eschew melody and harmony. Does all this stem in part from your serious interest in drumming, playing cymbals in the Yale Marching Band?

**AL:** Yes. Many of my recent works explore the phenomenon of acoustical beating, that is, bumps of sound produced when two or more closely tuned tones are sounded together. So in a sense you could say that there is plenty of rhythm in these pieces.

However, one of the great influences of playing cymbals and snare drums in the Yale Marching Band was the experience of starting to play in the highly reverberant tunnel of the Yale Bowl, then marching out onto the field and hearing that huge reflective space.

**AMK:** What an interesting memory. It immediately brings to mind *I Am Sitting in a Room* (1969), *Vespers* (1967), and *Chambers* (1968), and many other of your early compositions in which you explore the acoustical properties of a single space. Is that tunnel your earliest recollection of realizing how rich resonances could be, originating from inside a semi-enclosed chamber?

**AL:** That, and as a child putting a seashell up to my ear and listening to the sound of the ocean.

**AMK:** You have mentioned a little music store in Nashua that was a source of some of your early introduction to classical music.

**AL:** It was called Nutting's, and it sold musical instruments, sheet music and a few recordings  I remember going in there at the age of maybe thirteen or fourteen, and finding a record of the Schoenberg *Serenade*—can you believe that? I remember buying it and playing it, and saying to myself, "*What is this?*" It came as a complete surprise. I also bought a recording of Virgil Thomson's *Portraits*.

The Grieg *Piano Concerto* was the first real classical piece I can recall. At home we didn't listen to classical music that much. Gershwin's *Rhapsody in Blue* was my father's idea of what an American composer should be writing, and rightly so I think. But I was more interested in jazz and big band music. Then I remember getting a record of Beethoven's *Fifth Symphony* and thought it was amazingly beautiful. And somehow I knew I was being a little bit snobby climbing a rung above my family's taste, although in no way would I ever knock that taste. And I remember falling in love with Brahms's *Symphony No. 4 in E Minor*. I must have played that record a thousand times. One summer I was a counselor at Camp Wonalancet, a boys' camp in New Hampshire. At lights out I would softly play this piece on my record player while my campers were falling asleep. I wonder how many of them remember that?

**AMK:** I'm impressed with what an independent spirit you were. Your parents wanted you to study piano, but you insisted on playing the drums. Obviously you were smart, but you were not a great student in high school. In fact, after graduation you needed a remedial "gap year" to get into college.

**AL:** I never studied in high school, so my grades were bad. After graduation most of my school chums were going off to college. I didn't get into college, and when that became evident, my mother sent me up to the Nashua Public Library to find a preparatory school for a post-graduate year. I was reading James Joyce at that time, *Portrait of an Artist as a Young Man*, and I had the romantic notion to go to college in Ireland. Anyway, I looked up American preparatory schools, and the two that caught my attention were Canterbury and Portsmouth Priory. I can't fathom why; I was at that point not very religious. The next morning my mother picked up the telephone and called The Priory School in Rhode Island and enrolled me in the summer program. She was strong-willed enough to push at the very moment my life might have gone the wrong way. I stayed through the next year and by spring I had done well enough to get accepted to Dartmouth and Yale.

Most of my pieces are built on physical or acoustical principles that you can talk about—alpha waves, echoes, resonances, things of that kind. But they become interesting, for me anyway, when you can't talk about them anymore.[6]

25

**AMK:** So off you went to Portsmouth Priory in 1949, an excellent boarding school run by an English order of the Benedictines, located on Narragansett Bay in Rhode Island. I assume it was still a nearly all-male enclave back then, emphasizing the classics and offering a lot of structure?

**AL:** Boarding schools are confined atmospheres. You have to stay in your room at night to study. The level of classroom work at Portsmouth was rigorous. The teachers were strict, but not like the Jesuits. Benedictines were more benign. It had a scholarly atmosphere, and you knew the dedicated faculty, made up of both monks and lay people, wanted you to strive for the best. They respected the boys. It was just wonderful. It was the first time in my life I understood a bit of mathematics. I got a glimpse of how to measure the area under a curve. We also studied Euclidean geometry.

There was an artist who lived in a little house on the edge of campus. I don't remember her affiliation with the school, but she would invite certain students over to her house and would rant and rave against sentimentality in art! I'll never forget that.

**AMK:** And that's where you observed a Trappist monk in the act of contemplation?

**AL:** It was during a school break. I'd done something wrong and they kept me over a couple of days. I don't know why, I was always getting into trouble. A nearby Trappist monastery had burned down, and the monks came over to live in the Portsmouth dormitories.

I remember going into the chapel and watching this Trappist monk in the act of contemplation. He wasn't praying the way I remembered pious parish priests prayed. He wasn't pious at all. I got the idea that he was simply thinking. I went back a couple of hours later and he was in the same kneeling position. I thought if there's any such thing as pure thought, this man was doing it. Pure thought would have to be thinking about something specific, without tension or argument. With contemplation one focuses the mind on some thing or idea; with meditation one is supposed to empty the mind. That experience has stayed with me all my life.

**AMK:** I think I know where you are going…

**AL:** Yes, when I perform my brain wave piece, *Music for Solo Performer* (1965), it is essential to sit and try not to think of anything, because if you create a visual image in your mind your alpha will block. That's meditation, isn't it? So my experiences with meditation (and contemplation) prepared me for *Solo Performer*. The two go together very well.

Mysticism, scholasticism, contemplation and this wonderful woman telling us not to be sentimental about art, plus singing Gregorian chant everyday formed me in important ways. Many of my pieces are ritualistic, too. *Vespers* (1967), for example, refers not only to the common bat of North America, but also to one of the eight monastic offices, recited just before dark. My works are very simple, clear and stripped bare. If I start with eight components, I usually condense it to four, then two. Finally I discover I can make do with one.

**AMK:** Portsmouth Priory was the boot camp that got you into Yale. Your father would have preferred that you attend his alma mater, Dartmouth, but you chose Yale.

**AL:** Yes. Yale had a School of Music and Dartmouth did not.

**AMK:** It was there that you really buckled down and learned music. Did you enter Yale planning to major in music?

**AL:** It was in my mind, although at the time I vacillated between music and law.

**AMK:** After graduating from Yale in 1954, you went straight into graduate study at Yale School of Music. By then you were an ardent Stravinsky-ite. But you chose to leave Yale?

I always say to my students at the first class: "I'm not interested in your opinions….I'm interested in your perceptions. So don't hear a piece and decide. That doesn't interest me, whether you think it's good or not. What did you hear? Tell me what you perceive." [8]

27

I like my music clean, like gin.[9]

I think it's built into my work that I don't succeed very well when I'm thinking in two dimensions; it's always more interesting when I'm thinking in terms of three-dimensional space. It's as if I've completely shifted into another gear. I just can't think of writing a melodic line....Sounds for me have to move not only up and down, but in and out, and across space somewhere; they have to live in space.[10]

**AL:** Music education in the United States at that time was very Eurocentric. Composers such as Harry Partch or John Cage were never mentioned. In fact Cage played at a residential college at Yale when I was there. He wasn't invited by the music department, and I didn't bother going. I just heard that somebody crazy was making noise with a typewriter (Erik Satie had used a typewriter in *Parade*, and Cage was simply using the idea.) I went to the Yale School of Music after graduating from Yale College, but dropped out after one year.

**AMK:** After leaving Yale School of Music, there are a few desultory years, traveling around the country when you were not studying music. Then back to New Haven. Your next stop, 1958, was Brandeis University, a very new school at that time. What drew you to Brandeis? You had left one of the very oldest universities in the country, and were now joining a newborn music department.

**AL:** I was living in New Haven, working at a department store. My friend, Stanley Mills, a PhD student in biochemistry at Yale, had been invited to do post-doctoral studies at Brandeis, and told me about the newly-formed music department there. Harold Shapero, Arthur Berger and Irving Fine were on the composition faculty. (Leonard Bernstein had just recorded Shapero's *Symphony for Classical Orchestra*.) They knew their Stravinsky better than anybody.

**AMK:** Are these the composers that Copland referred to as the American "Stravinsky school"?

**AL:** I think so. Berger, however, was moving toward serialism. I went up and had an interview with him. He was delighted to get a Yale student. I moved to Waltham, stayed for two years. I won a couple of prizes.

**AMK:** But first Tanglewood…

**AL:** Yes, during the summer of 1958, just before entering Brandeis, I went to Tanglewood. It was wonderful. You'd walk through the grounds and hear the Boston Symphony rehearsing.

At New Music Miami...there was

a panel and one of the critics said,

"I don't like wires." And I said,

"....In a piano, there are more than

88 of them."[11]

I had the job of recording the contemporary music concerts at ten o'clock on Sunday mornings. I used a Wollensak tape recorder. I remember recording Milton Babbitt's *Composition for Four Instruments*. Claudio Abbado and Zubin Mehta were in the conducting class. I studied composition with Lukas Foss. He was an ebullient teacher. Aaron Copland gave wonderful classes in orchestration. He was a generous musical presence. After a performance of my neoclassical flute and harpsichord partita, he exclaimed, "*Your music is so direct!*"

Once a week I would drive over from Tanglewood to Bruggerman's Hofbräu in the Catskills, and play drums in a little band consisting of pianist Dennis Miškiewicz, the grandson, I think, of the famous Polish poet. We also had an accordionist and a trumpet player. On Saturday nights, we'd play until one or two o'clock in the morning. Then I'd drive back to Tanglewood and sleep in my car, ready to cover my Sunday morning assignment.

I went back to Tanglewood for a second year and won the Jack E. Lund Prize.

**AMK:** Copland's remark "*Your music is so direct!*" was—perhaps inadvertently!— prescient. It succinctly describes just the kind of "scores" that would, over that next decade, win you wide acclaim: *Music for Solo Performer* (1965), *Vespers* (1967) and *I Am Sitting in a Room* (1969). And many, many others thereafter.

And you crossed paths with John Cage at Tanglewood?

**AL:** The first time I met him was when he offered me a ride in his VW bus at Tanglewood, in 1958 or 1959. I told him I was a composition student there. He asked me what kind of music I wrote. I answered flippantly, "*Way back in the 20th century.*" He replied, "*Well, our music is timeless!*"

Later, after I had returned from Rome, I participated in concerts organized by Charlotte Moorman at Judson Hall on 57th Street (New York City). Cage and

David Tudor gave a concert. It was exhilarating—the tangle of wires hanging down from Tudor's equipment tables!

**AMK:** Very soon after your arrival in Europe on a Fulbright you attended the now infamous 1960 Cage-Tudor concert at Teatro La Fenice in Venice. That is an often-acknowledged turning point for you. But what contributed to your being able to be so receptive to that event? (Most others there responded to it with great anger. It even rated a scathing review in *Time* magazine.)

**AL:** Actually I was one of the angry ones at the Fenice. I even remember yelling something like *"Johnny! Johnny!"* from the balcony. I am embarrassed to think about it now. However, this experience profoundly changed my way of thinking, particularly when I got home. Something about that concert broke through the malaise I was having as a neoclassic composer, knowing there was no future in it. Cage offered a real alternative.

**AMK:** Was it, in part, your friendship with John Cage that led you to join the music faculty at Wesleyan?

**AL:** Yes, John suggested it to Dick Winslow, chair of the Wesleyan music department at the time. Cage appreciated my having invited him to perform at the Rose Art Museum at Brandeis in 1965 where we premiered his *Rozart Mix* and my *Music for Solo Performer*. And when Dick sought John's advice about whom to hire for the experimental music position, he suggested me.

**AMK:** Looking back over the past four decades, generations of Wesleyan students have been very lucky that Dick Winslow turned to John Cage.

*Summer 2011*

**Notes**

**1** Alvin Lucier, interview by Robert Ashley, *Music with Roots in the Aether*, Program 3, 1976.

**2** Frank J. Otieri, "Sitting in a Room with Alvin Lucier," *NewMusicBox* (April 2005), from www.newmusicbox.org/articles/sitting-in-a-room-with-alvin-lucier-alvin-lucier.

**3** Alvin Lucier, interview with Max Brivic, *The Wesleyan Argus*, November 6, 2009: 3.

**4** Otieri, "Sitting in a Room."

**5** Nicolas Collins, "Ghosts and Monsters: Technology and Personality in Contemporary Music," *Leonardo Music Journal*: 8.5 (1998).

**6** William Duckworth, *20/20: 20 New Sounds of the 20th Century* (New York, NY: Schirmer Books, 1999), 117–118.

**7** Otieri, "Sitting in a Room."

**8** Ibid.

**9** Daniel Wolf, May 14, 2011 (12:01 am), "Alvin Lucier is 80," *http://renewablemusic.blogspot.com/2011/05/alvin-lucier-is-80*.html.

**10** Alvin Lucier and Douglas Simon, *Chambers* (Middletown, CT: Wesleyan University Press, 1980), 157.

**11** Otieri, "Sitting in a Room."

## Alvin Lucier Biography

Alvin Lucier, Wesleyan's John Spencer Camp Professor of Music, began teaching full-time at Wesleyan in 1970, and retired at the end of the spring 2011 semester.

He was born in 1931 in Nashua, New Hampshire, and was educated in local public and parochial schools and at the Portsmouth Abbey School in Rhode Island. Lucier studied music theory and composition at Yale University (BA '54) with Howard Boatwright, Richard Donvan, David Kraehenbuhl and Quincy Porter, and at Brandeis University (MFA '60) with Arthur Berger and Harold Shapero. During the summers of 1958 and 1959, Lucier studied at Tanglewood with Aaron Copland and Lukas Foss, and spent two years, 1960 to 1962, in Rome on a Fulbright Scholarship.

From 1962 to 1970, he taught at Brandeis and conducted the University Chamber Chorus, which devoted much of its time to new music. Lucier invited John Cage to perform in a 1965 concert at the university's Rose Art Museum, an occasion marked by the premiere of two subsequently iconic works: Cage's *Rozart Mix* and Lucier's *Music for Solo Performer* (his "brain wave" piece). In 1966, Robert Ashley, David Behrman, Gordon Mumma and Lucier founded the Sonic Art Union, and together toured widely for a decade, presenting individual works, sharing equipment and assisting each other.

Lucier has pioneered in many areas of music composition, performance and sound installations. Much of his work explores the physical properties of sound, often focusing on the resonances of spaces, both small and large. His recent works include compositions for solo instruments, chamber ensemble and orchestra in which, by means of close tunings with pure tones, sound waves are caused to spin through space. In 2000, the Whitney Museum presented an important survey, *I Am Sitting in a Room: American Sound Art 1950-2000*, using one of Lucier's best-known works in its title. He is married to Wendy Stokes, a psychiatric APRN and former dancer. They have a daughter, Amanda Lucier, who is a photojournalist. (A.M.K.)

Roland Dahinden, Alvin Lucier and
Hildegard Kleeb, in front of Sol LeWitt's
*Wall Drawing #730*, (1993)
Stadtgalerie Kiel, 1995
Photo credit: Helmut Kunde

# Concents

Commentary by Alvin Lucier

**Silver Streetcar for the Orchestra**, 1988
for solo amplified triangle
*Brian Johnson*, triangle

*Silver Streetcar for the Orchestra* is one of a series of pieces for conventional musical instruments I have been making since 1982. These include *Crossings*, for small orchestra with slow-sweep pure wave oscillator (1982–1984); *In Memoriam Jon Higgins*, for clarinet with slow-sweep pure wave oscillator (1984); *Septet for Three Winds, Four Strings and Pure Wave Oscillator* (1985); *Kettles*, for five timpani with two slow-sweep pure wave oscillators (1987) and *Fideliotrio*, for viola, cello and piano (1987–1988). All these works explore natural timbral and spatial characteristics of sound waves.

In *Silver Streetcar*, the player dampens the triangle with the thumb and forefinger of one hand while tapping the instrument with the other. The performance consists of moving the geographical locations of these two activities and changing the speed and loudness of the tapping. During the course of the performance, the acoustic characteristics of the folded metal bar are revealed.

*Silver Streetcar for the Orchestra* was written expressly for Brian Johnson. The title of the work was taken from the surrealist text, *Instrumentation* (1922), by Luis Buñuel.

**A Tribute to James Tenney**, 1986
for double bass
and pure wave oscillators
*Roy Wiseman*, double bass

Two pure wave oscillators are routed through a mixer to a pair of loudspeakers positioned on either side of the stage. The bassist stands equidistant between them.

During the performance the oscillators are tuned successively to five pairs of whole tones. Against each pair, the bassist plays a series of sustained tones,

33

tuning some of them microtonally, in steps of one-third of a semitone (33 cents). As he or she does so, audible beats are produced at speeds determined by the distances between the instrumentally and electronically generated tones. The farther apart, the faster the beating. At unison, no beating occurs. Furthermore, under certain conditions the beats may be heard to spin in elliptical patterns through space, from the higher source to the lower.

The oscillators are faded in and out for each pair of tunings. The letters preceding each pair give their stereo placement. Starting with the first pair, the upper and lower tones are panned to the left and right loudspeakers, respectively. For each successive tuning, the stereo is reversed.

This work was composed for *A Tribute to James Tenney,* a collection of music and writing honoring the composer, which appeared in *Perspectives of New Music*, Volume 25, numbers 1 & 2, Winter 1987 and Summer 1987. The original title was *Homage To James Tenney*. It was written expressly for bassist Roy Wiseman.

**In Memoriam Jon Higgins**, 1985
for clarinet and
slow-sweep pure wave oscillator
*Anthony Burr*, clarinet

In *In Memoriam Jon Higgins,* an electronically generated pure wave, flowing from a single loudspeaker, slowly sweeps through the range of the clarinet. As it does so, the clarinetist plays long tones across the ascending wave, creating interference patterns, beats of loud sound produced as the sound waves coincide. The speed of the beats is determined by the distance between the waves: the farther apart, the faster the beating. At unison, no beating occurs. At very close tunings—within a few cycles per second—the patterns may be heard to spin through space.

The pure wave sweeps one semitone every 30 seconds. The clarinetist is asked to hold each tone for one minute. Typically, the tone straddles the sweeping wave equidistant on either side. Occasionally a tone starts a minute before the wave reaches unison with it; once it starts at unison it is sustained until the wave rises a whole tone above it. Three times the tone steps up or down to meet the rising wave.

*In Memoriam Jon Higgins* was first performed by Thomas Ridenour in December of 1984 at the Connecticut Composers Festival at Real Art Ways, in Hartford, Connecticut.

**Panorama**, 1993
for trombone and piano
*Roland Dahinden*, trombone
*Hildegard Kleeb*, piano

In the spring of 1993, Roland Dahinden and Hildegard Kleeb gave me a panoramic photograph of the Swiss and Austrian Alps, seen from their hometown of Zug, Switzerland. I was planning a skiing trip to Switzerland and had asked them to bring me back some travel brochures. At the same time I was thinking about composing a piece for them. As soon as I saw that photograph I got the idea to transcribe the mountain ranges into musical notation. The trombonist would "draw" the mountains by sliding continuously—Dahinden is an expert skier—throughout the piece, breathing when necessary. The pianist would punctuate the mountain peaks. Since the sliding pitches of the trombone would seldom match exactly the fixed tones of the piano, the discrepancies would be heard as audible beats, bumps of sound that occur as sound waves coincide.

*Panorama* was written especially for Kleeb and Dahinden. I have had the pleasure of working with them on earlier occasions. In 1992 I composed *Music for Piano with One or More Snare Drums* for Ms. Kleeb who first performed it on March 21 of that year at the Galerie Sou-Sol in Geneva, Switzerland. Then on February 28, 1993, Roland Dahinden premiered *Stacks*, a site-specific work for solo trombone and a sculpture by Richard Serra, permanently installed in the Yale University Art Gallery in New Haven, Connecticut.

**Charles Curtis**, 2002
for cello and
slow-sweep pure wave oscillators
*Charles Curtis*, cello

During the course of the performance two pure wave oscillators sweep up and down from a central tone drawing the letter "C" twice. As the waves rise and fall, a cellist sustains double stopped long tones against the sweeping waves, creating audible beats at speeds determined by the closeness of the tunings.

The beating continually changes speed because the pure waves are in constant motion. If a player's tone begins before a pure wave reaches unison with it, the beating will start fast and slow down. If a tone starts at unison, the beating will start at zero, then speed up as the wave moves away from it. If a tone crosses unison, the beating will slow down, stop, then speed up again.

The cellist plays long tones of 2 or 3 bow lengths each, separated by silences. He is free to anticipate or delay his tones thereby changing the shapes of the beating patterns.

This piece was written for Charles Curtis. The pure wave sweeps were designed by Bob Bielecki and executed in Max MSP by Anne Wellmer.

**Still Lives**, 1995
for piano and
slow-sweep pure wave oscillators
*Joseph Kubera*, piano

| | |
|------|----------------|
| I | Diamond |
| II | Hammock |
| III | Barbeque Grill |
| IV | Lampshade |
| V | Two Floor Tiles |
| VI | Ferns |
| VII | Bread Knife |
| VIII | Chop Sticks |

When pianist Joseph Kubera asked me to compose a work for him, I decided to write a suite of eight short movements. For the shape of each movement I simply looked around my house and selected images and objects that came into my line of vision, including the hammock strung between two trees in my backyard and a pair of chop sticks lying on the kitchen counter. I drew the shapes on paper with precise timings and pitch information and sent them to Bob Bielecki who programmed them on a computer and recoded the waves on digital audio tape. I copied the shapes on music paper, then notated pitches for the piano that would cause audible beating: the near-unison and, because of their strong overtones, the near-octave and twelfth below the sounding waves. The piano tones are notated simultaneously with the waves against which they are to beat, but the pianist is free to anticipate or delay them, causing more varied forms of beating.

*Still Lives*, written from July 26 to August 20, 1995, was first performed by Kubera on March 18, 1999, in Merkin Hall, New York on the Interpretations Series.

**Music for Gamelan Instruments, Microphones, Amplifiers and Loudspeakers**, 1994

Wesleyan University

Gamelan Ensemble

*Sumarsam and I. M. Harjito*, Directors

In 1994, when Wesleyan University invited me to present a festival of my work, I decided to make as many new works as possible rather than simply present a retrospective of older works. I had for some time wanted to make a work for Javanese gamelan but was hesitant to do so for three reasons: one, I didn't want to infringe on the generosity of my colleagues Sumarsam and I. M. Harjito, who were so often asked to relinquish important rehearsal time for the performance of new works; two, I have always been wary of using someone else's music in my own work; and three, I didn't have an original idea. I certainly didn't want my piece to sound Indonesian. It wasn't until I started imagining the bowl-shaped *bonangs* of the gamelan orchestra as resonant chambers to be sounded more than objects to be struck that I felt I could make a work I could call my own. I now felt comfortable in asking my colleagues if they would be interested in having me compose a work for their ensemble. They agreed.

During the performance four players place *bonangs* of various sizes over microphones, creating feedback, the pitch of which is determined by the shape and size of the bowl and the resonant characteristics of the room. Three *gender* players strike the bars on their metallophones, searching for the pitches of the feedback strands. Since it is virtually impossible that a strand of feedback will match exactly on any fixed-pitch instrument, audible beats, or bumps of sounds occur. The closer the tuning, the slower the beating. When the players reach near-unison with a feedback strand they may slow down or speed up their playing, creating beating patterns between the pitches of their instruments and those of the feedback.

37

*Music for Gamelan Instruments* was first performed on October 18, 1994 in World Music Hall at Wesleyan University by the Wesleyan University Gamelan Ensemble.

**Six Geometries**, 1993

for chorus with

slow-sweep pure wave oscillators

Wesleyan University

Collegium Musicum

*Jane Alden*, Director

I    Small Fish Logo

II   The Letter X

III  Right Angle

IV  Triangle

V   The Figure 5

VI  Plums

My first idea was to set several of William Carlos Williams's poems for four-part chorus. I took an image from each of the poems and would "draw" that image with pure sound waves. The chorus would sing the words of the poems against the pure waves, creating beating patterns. I soon learned that the words got in the way of the acoustical phenomena, so I simply jettisoned them—beautiful though they were—and kept the shapes they left behind. Throughout the work the chorus sings an "oo" sound, which is close enough in timbre to a pure wave to create vivid beating patterns.

The form of each movement, with the exception of the first, was taken from an image in a poem by Williams. For example, in *Fine Work with Pitch and Copper*, men putting a new roof on a house lay down eight-foot strips of copper beaten at right angles. I simply took that image and programmed two pure waves to sweep in the form of a right angle. I drew the letter "X" from the word "saxifrage" in one of the poems; the figure 5, seen on the side of a fire engine in another; and the outline of plums in another. The title of the first movement, *Small Fish Logo*, refers to the symbols one sees on certain automobiles in America.

*Six Geometries* was commissioned by Eric Soderstrom and the Finnish Radio Choir. It was first performed in its entirety by the Wesleyan Chamber Choir, Eric Hung, Director, on October 22, 1994, in the final concert of the Alvin Lucier: Collaborations Festival.

**Shadow Lines**, 2008

*Anthony Burr*, clarinet

*Charles Curtis*, cello

*Roland Dahinden*, trombone

*Tony Lombardozzi*, electric guitar

*Roy Wiseman*, double bass

*Shadow Lines* is one of a series of works for solo and instrumental ensembles in which players closely tune long tones in order to produce audible beats—bumps of sound—that occur when sound waves coincide. The closer the tuning the slower the beating; at unison no beating occurs, connecting with my fascination with the idea that pitch can create rhythm.

During the course of the performance an electric guitar, cello and double bass slowly sweep up and down, scanning the interval of a major third. As they do so, a clarinet and trombone play single tones against the sweeping waves, creating audible beats that continually slow down, stop and speed up as the string tones approach, pass through and leave the sustained wind tones.

*Shadow Lines* was commissioned by the Quiet Music Ensemble in Cork, Ireland. The title was taken from Joseph Conrad's novel, *The Shadow-Line: A Confession*. The 15-minute work was completed on May 19, 2008, in Middletown, Connecticut.

**Panorama 2**, 2011

for trombone and thirteen strings

*Roland Dahinden*, trombone

members of the Wesleyan University Orchestra

*Angel Gil-Ordóñez*, Director

During the course of the performance the trombonist glisses up and down, drawing a part of the skyline of the Williams Fork mountain range, as viewed from Ute Peak, Colorado. As he does so the string players follow his sweeps at pitch levels above and below those of the trombone, copying the shape of his line as best they can.

*Panorama 2* was written for Roland Dahinden and was first performed by him and the orchestra of the Musikschule der Stadt Zug on January 28, 2011, in the Ref. Kirche, Zug, Switzerland.

**Exploration of the House**, 2005

for orchestra and digital tape delay system, Wesleyan University Orchestra

*Angel Gil-Ordóñez*, Director

*Po-wei Weng*, Conductor

Several phrases, taken from Beethoven's overture, *The Consecration of the House*, are played in chronological order by the orchestra. As each one is played it is recorded, stored in computer memory and played back into the hall several times. As the repetitive process progresses, the resonant frequencies of the hall are revealed.

This process is similar to the one used in *I Am Sitting in a Room* (1969) for voice and tape.

*The Consecration of the House* was composed by Beethoven in 1822 to celebrate the reopening of the Josephstädter Theatre in Vienna. *Exploration of the House* was first performed on August 23, 2005, in Ostrava, Czech Republic, by the Janáček Philharmonic Orchestra, Petr Kotik, Conductor.

**Lucier Celebration Concert III:**
**Recreation of *A Concert of Electronic Theatre Music May 3, 1968***
**Saturday, November 5, 2011**
**10pm**
**Memorial Chapel**

*The concert will be performed by the original performers: John Fullemann ('70), John Pemberton ('70), Douglas Simon ('69, MA '71) and Peter Zummo ('70, MA '75) together with current graduate and undergraduate students.*

**Cariddwen**, 1968
*John David Fullemann,*
*John Pemberton, Douglas Simon,*
Co-composers

*Cariddwen* was composed as a collaborative work on tape by John Fullemann, John Pemberton and Douglas Simon. The title refers to the Celtic goddess Cariddwen, mentioned in Robert Graves's book *The White Goddess*. The text was taken from the "With Kiss. Kriss Criss. Cross Kriss. Kiss Cross" section as it appears in James Joyce's *Finnegans Wake*.

**Vespers**, 1967
accoustic orientation by means
of echolocation
*Alvin Lucier*, Composer

In this work four players move around a darkened space carrying Sondols, hand-held pulse wave oscillators, which emit sharp, fast clicks whose repetition rate can be varied. The players beam the sounds to various parts of the room, bouncing them off the walls, floor and ceiling. As the pulses ricochet from one reflective surface to another, multiple echoes are produced and, over time, an acoustic signature of the room is revealed. The title, *Vespers*, refers to the common bat of

40

North America, of the family *Vespertilionidae*, an expert in the art of echolocation, and to the Catholic evening service.

*Vespers* was first performed at the 1967 ONCE Festival in Ann Arbor, Michigan.

**Distance**, 1961
*Toshi Ichiyanagi*, Composer

*Distance*, written by Toshi Ichiyanagi in 1961, requires any number of players to play their instruments from at least three meters away.

I  N  T  E  R  M  I  S  S  I  O  N

**Flying, or Possibly Crawling or Sitting Still**, 1971–1972
excerpt from *Burdocks*
*Christian Wolff,* Composer

*Flying* is one of 10 pieces that comprise *Burdocks*, written by Christian Wolff in 1971 and 1972. Each part is notated differently. Some use elaborate graphic notation, others are simply texts. Conventional staff notation is minimal. There are sections for professional musicians and other parts for unskilled players. You can play as many parts as you want. You may choose a director, or form a committee, or hold a meeting to decide which parts to play and who will play them. There is no conductor.

**Rozart Mix**, 1965
*John Cage,* Composer

The published score of *Rozart Mix* consists of correspondence between John Cage and Alvin Lucier, containing instructions about the construction of 88 tape loops of various lengths to be played on 12 tape recorders, each with its own amplifier and loudspeaker. In the margins of the typewritten letters, Cage drew various ways of splicing the taped fragments so as to physically create different attacks and decays of the juxtaposed sounds. Each loop was extended around its own microphone stand. The sound material on each loop could be anything, although Cage suggested a non-popular music version. If a loop splice broke it was to be repaired and put away for future use. *Rozart Mix* was first performed on May 5, 1965, at the Rose Art Museum at Brandeis University.

**Lucier Celebration Concert IV:**

*Tributes*

**Sunday, November 6, 2011**

**2pm**

**Crowell Concert Hall**

The concert will include compositions by Robert Ashley, David Behrman, Neely Bruce, Alvin Lucier, Gordon Mumma, Pauline Oliveros, and Christian Wolff performed by members of the Wesleyan music commmunity, the West End String Quartet, and Tom Buckner.

# Alvin Lucier
# (and His Artist Friends)

Andrea Miller-Keller, Guest Curator

## Exhibition Checklist

*The exhibition includes audio recordings, scores and album/CD artwork for most of the musical compositions included below. There are also selected works by other artists who have inspired or been inspired by Lucier's work, or exchanged ideas with the composer in meaningful ways.*

*Some of the artists referenced in this exhibition include: John Ashbery, Robert Ashley, Mei-mei Berssenbrugge, John Cage, Italo Calvino, Nicolas Collins, Robert Coover, Viola Farber, Jacqueline Gourevitch, Robert Irwin, Ronald Kuivila, Sol LeWitt, Lee Lozano, Mary Lucier, George Manupelli, Keith McDermott, Nam June Paik, Steve Paxton, Richard Serra, Richard Tuttle, Bill Viola, William Carlos Williams, Robert Wilson.*

*Additionally included are memorabilia and ephemera of historical interest in the life and career of Alvin Lucier. Only a representative sampling of these materials is included in this listing.*

*Asterisk * indicates these works will be performed during the weekend celebration.*

Compositions by Lucier in the exhibition, listed alphabetically

**Almost New York** (2001) for five flutes (one player) [24:18], notated score. Jacqueline Gourevitch, *"almost New York" (from the Terrain/in flight drawing series)* (1995), graphite on paper, 14" x 11", gift from the artist to Lucier on his seventieth birthday. CD with same image.

**Chambers: In Honor of Alvin Lucier, sound in large and small resonant environments** (1968), text-based score. This new version is a compilation of individual works, each submitted as a tribute to Lucier, by his former students. Lucier himself contributed the thimble (with audio of the Cologne Hauptbahnhof), a well-known component of his earlier *Chambers*. Ron Kuivila, professor of music at Wesleyan, and a former student of Lucier, organized this installation.

[Also on view: *Resonant Things* (1991), sixteen ink drawings of resonant objects drawn by Lucier, published by the Contemporary Arts Museum, Houston in the Bayou Books series, Ltd. Edition.]

**Clocker** (1978) for amplified clock, performer with galvanic skin response sensor and digital delay system [44:12], text and diagrammatic score. Lucier: *I first got the idea for* Clocker *in 1978. I wanted to make a work in which a performer could speed up and slow down time, stopping it, if possible, simply by thinking....I was reading Italo Calvino's* If on a winter's night a traveler. *Throughout the book I would come upon images and ideas that seemed remarkably close to those I used in this work. For example,* "The thing I'd like most in the world...is to make clocks run backward...No, with thought, by concentrating until I force time to move back."

**Ever Present** (2002) for flute, saxophone and piano [15:27], notated score. Commissioned by the Drescher-Okabe-Armbruster Trio. Color photograph of *Getty Central Gardens*. Lucier first visited artist Robert Irwin's *Getty Gardens* in Los Angeles in 2002. Lucier used aspects of Irwin's graceful design, viewed from an angle, as the formal structure for this composition. The title is taken from two inscriptions Irwin placed at the entrance to his gardens: *EVER PRESENT, NEVER TWICE THE SAME* and *EVER CHANGING, NEVER LESS THAN WHOLE.*

**I Am Sitting in a Room** (1969) for voice and electromagnetic tape [15:32] (original short version), text-based score. First performed at the Guggenheim Museum, New York City in 1970 and originally accompanied by Mary Lucier's *Polaroid Slide Series*.

North Gallery is dedicated to the reception, impact and history of this landmark work, including examples of its widespread influence on other artists: original album cover, with Polaroids by Mary Lucier on both front and verso; artist's book by Laura van Eeden, *"I am sitting in a room"* (2011) 11" x 8.5", unfolded (Lucier Collection); unknown Spanish artist, *Sentadae en una Habitación* (n.d.), cartoon drawing from newspaper (Lucier Collection); and others.

Also a selection of works posted on YouTube and Vimeo, including Jon Christopher Nelson, *Dhoormages: I Am Sitting In A ...* (2001); Lev "Ljova" Zhubrin, *Klezmer Wake (They Are Sitting in a Room)* (2006); "Canzona" (Patrick Liddell), *I Am Sitting in a Video Room* (2007–2010); "McKack" (Kim Rubin), *I Am Sitting in a Room: Linguistic Version* (2010); and others.

In 2000, the Whitney Museum of American Art titled a major survey exhibition *I Am Sitting in a Room: American Sound Art, 1950–2000.*

**\*Music for Gamelan Instruments, Microphones, Amplifiers and Loudspeakers** (1994) [15:05]. This work features various sizes of bowl-shaped *bonang*, traditional to Indonesian gamelan orchestras, more as resonant chambers than as objects to be struck. Instruments include assorted *bonang*, 3 *genders*, 4 microphones, amplifiers and loudspeakers. The work is dedicated to Sumarsam and I.M. Harjito and has been performed throughout the United States and Indonesia.

**Music for Pure Waves, Bass Drums, and Acoustic Pendulums** (1980). A single sound wave flows through loudspeakers positioned behind four standing bass drums. As they do so, ping-pong balls, suspended in front of the drums, are caused to bounce away from the drumheads in unpredictable ways.

**Music for Solo Performer** (1965) for enormously amplified brain waves and percussion [39:14], (from Robert Ashley's *The Music of Alvin Lucier*, see below), a text-based score, and additional documentation on the history of this innovative piece. Lucier: *This work employs a configuration of electro-encephalographic (EEG) devices that generate alpha waves in real time, which resonate a large battery of percussion instruments.*

**Navigation for Strings** (1992) for string quartet [14:58] notated score (LeWitt Collection, Chester, Connecticut). The *Navigation for Strings* score was a gift from Lucier to Sol LeWitt, in exchange for LeWitt's *Wall Drawing #724* (1993), currently installed in the foyer of Lucier's home.

**On the carpet of the leaves illuminated by the moon** (2000) for koto or cello and pure wave oscillator [11:43]. This title is taken from the title of a chapter in Italo Calvino's novel *If on a winter's night a traveler:* "The gingko

leaves fell like rain from the boughs and dotted the lawn with yellow. I was walking with Mr. Okeda on the path of smooth stones. I said I would like to distinguish the sensation of each single gingko leaf from the sensation of all others, but I was wondering if it would be possible...."

**Outlines of Persons and Things** (1975) on *Landscape with Alvin Lucier* (see below), as the background in an interview of Lucier with Robert Ashley. *Part 3* of Ashley's *Music with Roots in the Aether* (1976) [57:40], with text-based score. Filmed in Wesleyan's Crowell Concert Hall.

**\*Panorama** (1993) for trombone and piano [15:48], notated score. Panoramic black and white photograph of the Swiss and Austrian Alps, gift to Lucier from musicians Roland Dahinden and Hildegard Kleeb. Lucier: *As soon as I saw the photograph I got the idea to transcribe the mountain ranges into musical notation.*

This "tourist" photograph also became the basis for Sol LeWitt's *Wall Drawing #730*: wall drawing instructions, black and white and color photographs. Also, Lucier's certificate of ownership for LeWitt Wall Drawing #724, gift by exchange. (*See Navigation for Strings* above.) Catalogue: *Alvin Lucier and Sol LeWitt/Chambers.* [Knut Nievers, Erich de Visscher, Daniel Wolf and Stadtgalerie Kiel. *Chambers: Alvin Lucier, Sol LeWitt.* (Stadtgalerie Kiel, 1995).]

**Panorama 2** (2011) for trombone and 13 strings [14:00], notated score. This composition, based on the panoramic skyline as shown at this website, http://www.rockymountainscenery.com/qtvr/ute/panorama.html, scans the elevation of the Colorado mountain range that includes Ute Peak in the Williams Fork Mountains on the Summit/Grand County Line (elevation

12,303 feet). Lucier spends a month each summer with his family at their trailer on the Williams Fork River.

**The Queen of the South** (1972) for players, responsive surfaces, strewn material and closed circuit television systems, text-based score, [time indeterminate]. This DVD was filmed by Bill Viola, *Art Tapes 22*, Florence, 1972 [30:00].

**SKIN, MEAT, BONE, the Wesleyan Project** (1994) in collaboration with director Robert Wilson and actor Keith McDermott, on DVD [19:19]. Excerpts from the Wesleyan performance, November 5, 1994.

**Theme** (1994) for four voices and sonorous vessels, text based on a poem by John Ashbery [18:45]. Text of Ashbery's *Theme* (n.d.) is on a nearby wall. The poem is recited by four speakers into various resonant objects such as milk bottles, shells, ostrich eggs, etc. The speakers attempt to allow the resonances of their own voices to match those of the objects into which they speak.

**Wave Songs** (1998), eleven solos for female voice and pure wave oscillators [18:00]. This work was commissioned by the Wadsworth Atheneum for a 1998 exhibition of the works of visual artist Lee Lozano that included her eleven *Wave Paintings* (1967–70). The series, based loosely on the physics of light, depicts waves in increasing numbers, from two to 96, each in a different muted monochrome. Lucier: *An oscillator is a simple electronic device that can be tuned accurately and emit a steady sound for an indefinite period of time. In each solo the oscillators are tuned relative to the size of the waves in one of Lee Lozano's Wave Paintings. Throughout the work the singer sings against the oscillator tones creating audible beats — bumps of sound as the sound waves coincide. I imagine the work as a mini opera, with the singer taking the part of the* *artist, singing her paintings into existence or perhaps simply humming to herself as she worked on them.*

### Other works in the exhibition

**Robert Ashley**, *Opera for Television: Music with Roots in the Aether Part 3* (1976), including *Landscape with Alvin Lucier*, an interview by Ashley with Lucier (see above).

**George Manupelli**, *Dr. Chicago Trilogy*, excerpts from three films: *Dr. Chicago* (1968); *Ride Dr. Chicago Ride* (1970); *Cry Dr. Chicago* (1971), all starring Alvin Lucier as Dr. Chicago, with Mary Ashley, Steve Paxton and others. Official website: georgemanupelli.com. These three films were recently among the first group of experimental films selected to be restored by the American Film Institute. George Stevens, Jr., Founder/Director, AFI: "*Dr. Chicago is the next American folk hero.*"

**Nam June Paik, *Double Portrait: John Cage and Alvin Lucier*** (c. 1975), collage: two playing cards mounted and framed, 8" x 10".

**Photographs:** More than 40 archival photographs are part of the exhibition, including: *Young Lucier and His Father at a Rotary Dinner in Nashua, NH* (c. 1937); *Lucier as Riflery Instructor, Riflery Range with Campers, Camp Wonalancet, NH* (c. 1948); *Graduation from Yale '54 in Marching Band Regalia, with Mother; Lucier Receiving Prize from Aaron Copland, Tanglewood Residency* (c. 1959); *Lucier Preparing Equipment for* Music for Solo Performer (1964); *Lucier (conductor) at Karlheinz Stockhausen's U.S. Premiere of* Originale *with Allen Ginsberg, Allan Kaprow (director), Mary Bauermeister, Robert Breer at Judson Hall, NYC,* (1964); *Restaurant Menu with Photograph of Cast of* Dr. Chicago *and Bob Ashley at Dinner* (c.1969); *Lucier and John Cage Blowing Up Balloons for Performance of Christian Wolff's 1964 Composition,* For 1, 2, or 3 People

(1988); and *Wendy Stokes and Alvin Lucier Peering through* Chinese Space, *Richard Tuttle's Sculpture for Performance Work with Mei-mei Berssenbrugge and Lucier* (1994).

**Ephemera:** Noteworthy concert programs, articles, reviews, etc.

**Objects:** Brain wave amplifier; Sondols; toy crickets; tapes from the original performance of John Cage's *Rozart Mix\** (1965); *Notes in the Margins*, program book, hand-written by Alvin Lucier, for the re-creation of the 1965 concert at Brandeis University for the "John Cage at Wesleyan Symposium" (1988); Edmund Catchpool, and John Satterly, *A Textbook of Sound* (c.1894/7th ed.,1949); Donald R. Griffin, *Echoes of Bats and Men* (1959); Hans Jenny, *Cymatics: A Study of Wave Phenomena & Vibration* (1967); Calvin R. Graf, *Listen to Radio Energy, Light and Sound* (1978); Lawrence Wechsler, *Seeing Is Forgetting the Name of the Thing One Sees: A Life of Contemporary Artist Robert Irwin* (1982); works of literature related to compositions by Lucier, etc.

# Biographies

**Jane Alden**, musicologist, is associate professor of music at Wesleyan University and author of *Songs, Scribes and Society: The History and Reception of the Loire Valley Chansonniers* (Oxford University Press, 2010). Her ongoing research addresses both medieval and experimental music.

**Robert Ashley**, composer, is co-founder of the ONCE Festivals of contemporary music and the Sonic Arts Union, and former director of the Center for Contemporary Music at Mills College (1969–1981). His work in new forms of opera and multi-disciplinary performance are acknowledged classics of language in a musical setting.

**David Behrman**, composer and designer of multimedia installations, teaches at the Bard College Milton Avery Graduate School of the Arts and contributes music to the Merce Cunningham Dance Company. He was a co-founder, with Robert Ashley, Alvin Lucier and Gordon Mumma, of the Sonic Arts Union.

**Anthony Braxton**, recipient of a MacArthur Fellowship (1994), is a composer, saxophonist, clarinettist, flautist, pianist and philosopher. He is professor of music at Wesleyan University, director of the Tri-Centric Foundation and has released well over a hundred albums.

**Neely Bruce**, composer, conductor, pianist and scholar, is professor of music and American studies at Wesleyan University. His catalog of works include over 250 songs and 5 operas, and he was the first pianist ever to perform the entire song oeuvre of Charles Ives (as part of the Ives Vocal Marathon).

**Anthony Burr**, clarinettist, is a leading interpreter of contemporary music. Assistant professor of music at the University of California, San Diego, he has collaborated with Laurie Anderson, Alvin Lucier, John Zorn, Charles Curtis and experimental filmmaker Jennifer Reeves.

**Thomas Buckner**, baritone and recipient of the American Music Center's Letter of Distinction (1996), is widely recognized for his rich contribution as an innovative performer, producer and promoter of some of the most adventurous music of the 20th century.

**Nicolas Collins** ('76, MA '79) is professor in the Department of Sound at the School of the Art Institute of Chicago. He is editor-in-chief of the *Leonardo Music Journal* and author of *Handmade Electronic Music: The Art of Hardware Hacking* (Routledge, 2006/2009).

**Charles Curtis**, cellist, is a celebrated soloist and ensemble player. Professor of contemporary music performance at the University of California, San Diego, he has just recorded La Monte Young's *Trio for Strings* in a new just-intonation version.

**Roland Dahinden** (MA '94) is a composer and performer who specializes in the performance of new music and improvisation. He has performed works written for him by Anthony Braxton, John Cage, Alvin Lucier, Pauline Oliveros and Christian Wolff, and collaborated with visual artists like Inge Dick and Sol LeWitt.

**Andrew Raffo Dewar** (MA '04, PhD '09) is a composer, improviser, woodwind instrumentalist and ethnomusicologist with expertise in experimental sound art. He is now assistant professor of interdisciplinary arts at New College and School of Music, University of Alabama.

**John Fullemann** ('70), currently designs specialized electronic equipment for the Corelatus Company, Stockholm. For many years he was technical director for the Merce Cunningham Dance Company. His collaborations include working with Alvin Lucier on *Solar Sounder I*.

**Angel Gil-Ordóñez**, internationally renowned conductor, is the music director of the Post-Classical Ensemble in Washington, D.C. and director of orchestral studies at Wesleyan University. In 2006, he was awarded Spain's highest civilian decoration, the Royal Order of Queen Isabella.

**Hauke Harder**, composer and molecular physics researcher (PhD, Physics, University of Kiel '93) began composing in 1989 with a key interest in pure intervals. He co-founded Material Press with Daniel James Wolf in 1992 and has been assisting Lucier on installation projects since 1995. He co-directed the documentary film about Lucier, *No Ideas But In Things* (2012).

**I. M. Harjito** is a performer, teacher, and composer of Javanese gamelan. A graduate of Indonesia's State Conservatory for the Traditional Performing Arts, Harjito has worked with one of the major figures of 20th-century Javanese music, Martopangrawit, and has since directed gamelan ensembles in Australia, Canada, Indonesia and the United States.

**Toshi Ichiyanagi**, composer of Japanese avant-garde music, studied at New York's Juilliard Conservatory, where he met John Cage and began experimenting with electronic music. Ichiyanagi composes for both Western and Japanese instruments. He is a recipient of the Suntory Music Award (2001) and Japan's Order of Culture.

**Brian Johnson**, percussionist, is an international soloist and ensemble musician. He has premiered works by leading figures of the American avant-garde, including John Cage, Alvin Lucier, Joseph Celli and Stuart Saunders Smith.

**Hildegard Kleeb**, pianist, specializes in the performance of new music and improvisation, and teaches at the Muzikschule der Stadt Zug, Switzerland. She has an extensive discography, and recently worked on a series of social performance projects.

**Joseph Kubera**, pianist, is a leading interpreter of contemporary music. He is a core member of the S.E.M. Ensemble, the Downtown Ensemble and Roscoe Mitchell's New Chamber Ensemble. Solo recordings include Beth Anderson's *Piano Concerto*, Cage's *Music of Changes*, Lucier's *Still Lives* and Cowell's *Nine Ings*.

**Ronald Kuivila** ('77), university professor and chair of the music department, composer and sound artist, has been teaching at Wesleyan

University since 1981. He has an extensive discography and his sound installations and concert music are presented internationally.

**Richard Lerman**, composer and sound artist, is professor at the New College of Interdisciplinary Arts & Sciences, Arizona State University. His work uses custom-made contact microphones of unusually small sizes to record environmental sounds not easily heard (or noticed).

**Tony Lombardozzi**, guitarist, has performed extensively with legends of jazz such as Clark Terry, Kenny Barron, Bill Barron, Ed Blackwell, Bill Watrous and Milt Hinton. He has been on the Wesleyan University music faculty since 1986. Since 1997, Lombardozzi has recorded and performed internationally with Jazz Vocalist Giacomo Gates.

**Paula Matthusen**, composer and assistant professor of music at Wesleyan University, writes both acoustic and experimental electroacoustic music, performs frequently with Ouisaudei, Groundwave New Music Collective, Object Collection and Winter Company, utilizing percussion, live processing and analog electronics.

**Andrea Miller-Keller**, guest curator of *Alvin Lucier (and His Artist Friends)*, worked at the Wadsworth Atheneum Museum of Art from 1969 to 1998. Miller-Keller was the founding curator of *MATRIX, a changing exhibition of contemporary art* (the proto-type for over 60 programs nation-wide). She has organized over 150 exhibitions, including the first retrospective of Sol LeWitt wall drawings, was a co-curator of the 2000 Whitney Biennial, and continues to lecture, curate and write.

**Gordon Mumma**, composer, and co-founder of the ONCE Festivals of contemporary music and the Sonic Arts Union, was professor of music at the University of California, Santa

Cruz (1975–1994). In 2000, he received the John Cage Award from the Foundation for Contemporary Arts.

**Pauline Oliveros**, composer, performer and humanitarian, is Distinguished Research Professor of Music at Rensselaer Polytechnic Institute, Troy, New York, and Darius Milhaud Artist-in-Residence at Mills College, Oakland, California. Her work makes use of improvisation, electronic composition, ritual and meditation.

**Nam June Paik** (1932-2006), a Korean-born American artist, studied composition and music history in Germany where he met Karlheinz Stockhausen, John Cage and Joseph Beuys. In New York, he was an active participant in Fluxus and an early and widely-influential pioneer of video art, expanding that field to include both performance and installation pieces.

**John Pemberton** ('70, MA '72), is now associate professor of anthropology at Columbia University. His book *On the Subject of "Java"* (Cornell University Press, 1994) and other publications explore the peculiar relationships between culture and politics in Indonesia.

**Michael S. Roth** ('78) became the 16th president of Wesleyan University in 2007. He is a graduate of Wesleyan and received his PhD in history from Princeton University in 1984. From 2000 to 2007 Roth served as President of the California College of the Arts. Author of five books, Roth describes his scholarly interests as centered on "how people make sense of the past."

**Viola Rusche**, director of *Amor Vati* (2006) and *No Ideas But In Things* (2012), a film portrait of Lucier, is also a visual artist and film editor of several documentaries about artists.

**Douglas Simon** ('69, MA '71) owns and operates Studio Consultants, a New York firm engaged in the acoustic and electronic design of recording studios. He is co-author, with Alvin Lucier, of *Chambers*, a collection of scores and interviews (Wesleyan University Press, 1980).

**Mark Slobin**, ethnomusicologist, is Richard K. Winslow Professor of Music at Wesleyan University. A past president of the Society for Ethnomusicology and of the Society for Asian Music, Slobin has written extensively on East European Jewish music and the world of klezmer.

**Volker Straebel**, musicologist, works on electroacoustic music, the American and European avant-garde, intermedia, performance and sound art. He is co-director of the Electronic Music Studio at the Technische Universität and teaches Sound Studies at the Universität der Künste, Berlin.

**Sumarsam** (MA '76), ethnomusicologist, is university professor of music at Wesleyan University and author of *Gamelan: Cultural Interaction and Musical Development in Central Java* (University of Chicago Press, 1995). His areas of expertise include Indonesian music and theater, focusing on the performance, history and theory of gamelan and wayang. He is currently researching Islam in Indonesian performing arts for his second book.

**Pamela Tatge** ('84, MALS '10) is director of the Center for the Arts at Wesleyan University, which supports the academic departments in music, dance, theater and visual arts and commissions and presents artists. In 2010, she was awarded the William Dawson Award for Programmatic Excellence and Sustained Achievement in Programming from the Association for Performing Arts Presenters.

**Catherine Waters**, book designer, has won numerous design awards including the *Frances Smyth-Ravenel Prize for Excellence* from the American Association of Museums in 2010. She received her BA from the Hartford Art School, her MFA from Yale University.

**Roy Wiseman** has recorded and performed extensively as a double bassist. He is the artistic director of the New World Consort and the New World Jazz Orchestra, leads the "Elite Syncopation" quintet and is a long-standing member of the Wesleyan University music faculty.

**Daniel Wolf** (MA '85, PhD '90), composer and writer, is director of the Frankfurt-based publisher Material Press. He has written extensively about musical intonation and speculative music theory, especially the interaction between tuning systems and tonal musics.

**Christian Wolff**, internationally renowned composer, professor of classics and music at Dartmouth College (1971–1999). He is a member of the Akademie der Künste in Berlin, Germany and the American Academy of Arts & Sciences in Cambridge, Massachusetts.

**Peter Zummo** ('70, MA '75), composer and trombonist, has collaborated with composers and musicians ranging from Jon Lurie to Earle Brown. His compositions have been performed worldwide. His numerous works for dance include commissions from the choreographers Trisha Brown and David Dorfman as well as multiple collaborations with Stephanie Woodard (MA '74).

## Acknowledgments

We gratefully acknowledge the funders whose generosity has made this festival, symposium and exhibition possible, including many departments at Wesleyan University: Academic Affairs, the Allbritton Center for the Study of Public Life, Center for the Arts, the Music Department, the Lemberg Fund, University Relations and Wesleyan University Press.

Many people collaborated to make this celebration possible. In particular, we thank our guest curator, Andrea Miller-Keller, for her expertise and dedication in making the exhibition and this catalog a reality. Thanks are also due to our hard-working colleagues in the Department of Music led by Ron Kuivila and Jane Alden who organized the festival concerts, the symposium and film screenings, and to Su Zheng, Dan St. Clair and Deb Shore who gave them full support; to the industrious CFA staff: Lee Berman (Gallery Manager), John Elmore (who designed the exhibition), Erinn Roos-Brown (who coordinated this publication), Barbara Ally, Kyle Beaudette, Andy Chatfield, Mark Gawlak, Hanna Oravec, Camilla Parente, Bob Russo and CFA Interns Anya Backlund '11, Joanna Bourain '12 and Caitlin Colasacco '11; to Suzy Taraba for her tremendous efforts and Alec McLane and Pat Tully at the Wesleyan University Library; to Suzanna Tamminen (who invited us to produce this catalog) and our colleagues at Wesleyan University Press; to Melissa Datre, Allynn Wilkinson and Philip Issacs at the Wesleyan's ITS New Media Lab; to Clare Rogan, curator of Davison Art Center; to Anne Rhodes, research archivist at Oral History of American Music, Yale University; to Janet Passehl, curator of the LeWitt Collection, and Sofia LeWitt of the LeWitt Estate; and to Jonathan Hiam, curator of American Music, New York Public Library. Our appreciation also to Wesleyan's President Michael Roth, Ron Kuivila and Nic Collins for their important contributions to this catalog, and to Provost Rob Rosenthal and former Dean of the Arts and Humanities Krishna Winston, for their special support. Our gratitude to the designer of this catalog Catherine Waters, whose gift is seen on every page.

Most of all, we thank Alvin for the considerable time, energy and patience he has graciously offered, along with his wife Wendy Stokes, in providing us with the research materials and guidance we needed along the way. (P.T.)